Loving to Learn

The Commitment to Learning Assets

by Pamela Espeland and Elizabeth Verdick

free spirit
PUBLISHING®

Helping kids
help themselves™
since 1983

Library of Congress Cataloging-in-Publication Data
Espeland, Pamela.
    Loving to learn : the commitment to learning assets / by Pamela Espeland and Elizabeth Verdick.
        p. cm.—(The adding assets series for kids; bk. 5)
    Includes index.
    ISBN-13: 978-1-57542-183-4
    ISBN-10: 1-57542-183-6
1. Motivation in education—Juvenile literature. 2. Learning—Juvenile literature. I. Verdick, Elizabeth. II. Title. III. Series.
    LB1065.E835 2005
    370.15'4—dc22   2005021793

At the time of this book's publication, all facts and figures cited are the most current available; all telephone numbers, addresses, and Web site URLs are accurate and active; all publications, organizations, Web sites, and other resources exist as described in this book; and all have been verified as of July 2005. The author and Free Spirit Publishing make no warranty or guarantee concerning the information and materials given out by organizations or content found at Web sites, and we are not responsible for any changes that occur after this book's publication. If you find an error or believe that a resource listed here is not as described, please contact Free Spirit Publishing. Parents, teachers, and other adults: We strongly urge you to monitor children's use of the Internet.

Search Institute℠ and Developmental Assets™ are trademarks of Search Institute.

The original framework of 40 Developmental Assets (for adolescents) was developed by Search Institute © 1997, Minneapolis, MN 1-800-888-7828; *www.search-institute.org*. The Developmental Assets framework is used under license from Search Institute.

The FACTS! (pages 9, 24, 39, 55, and 69) are from *Coming into Their Own: How Developmental Assets Promote Positive Growth in Middle Childhood* by Peter C. Scales, Arturo Sesma Jr., and Brent Bolstrom (Minneapolis: Search Institute, 2004).

Illustrated by Chris Sharp
Cover design by Marieka Heinlen
Interior design by Crysten Puszczykowski
Index by Ina Gravitz

10 9 8 7 6 5 4 3 2 1
Printed in the United States of America

Free Spirit Publishing Inc.
217 Fifth Avenue North, Suite 200
Minneapolis, MN 55401-1299
(612) 338-2068
help4kids@freespirit.com
www.freespirit.com

Printed on recycled paper
including 30%
post-consumer waste

Contents

Introduction

If you knew ways to make your life better, right now and for the future, would you try them?

We're guessing you would, and that's why we wrote this book. It's part of a series of eight books called the **Adding Assets Series for Kids.**

What Are Assets, Anyway?

When we use the word **assets**, we mean good things you need in your life and yourself.

We don't mean houses, cars, property, and jewelry—assets whose value is measured in money. We mean **Developmental Assets** that help you to be and become your best. Things like a close, loving family. A neighborhood where you feel safe. Adults you look up to and respect. And (sorry!) doing your homework.

There are 40 Developmental Assets in all. This book is about adding five of them to your life. They're called the **Commitment to Learning Assets** because they're about being serious about school and other kinds of learning. A *commitment* is a promise you make to yourself or someone else. A commitment to learning is a promise to do your best in school, learn new things, do your homework, care about your teachers, and read—not just when you have to, but because you want to. If you like, you can make this promise to your parents, other family grown-ups, and your teachers. But it's most important to promise *yourself* to be a good learner.

The Commitment to Learning Assets	
Asset Name	**What It Means**
Achievement Motivation	You want to do well in school, and you try your best.
Learning Engagement	You like to learn new things in and out of school.
Homework	You usually hand in your homework on time.
Bonding to Adults at School	You care about and feel connected to the teachers and other adults at your school.
Reading for Pleasure	You like to read, and you read for fun on most days of the week.

Other books in the series are about the other 35 assets.* That may seem like a lot, but don't worry. You don't have to add them all at once. You don't have to add them in any particular order. But the sooner you can add them to your life, the better.

---

* If you're curious to know what the other assets are, you can read the whole list on pages 83–84.

Why You Need Assets

An organization called Search Institute surveyed hundreds of thousands of kids and teens across the United States. Their researchers found that some kids have a fairly easy time growing up, while others don't. Some kids get involved in harmful behaviors or dangerous activities, while others don't.

What makes the difference? Developmental Assets! Kids who have them are more likely to do well. Kids who don't have them are less likely to do well.

Maybe you're thinking, "Why should I have to add my own assets? I'm just a kid!" Because kids have the power to make choices in their lives. You can choose to sit back and wait for other people to help you, or you can choose to help yourself. You can also work with other people who care about you and want to help.

Many of the ideas in this book involve working with other people—like your parents, grandparents, aunts, uncles, and other family grownups. And your teachers, neighbors, coaches, Scout leaders, and religious leaders. They can all help add assets for you and with you.

It's likely that many of the adults in your life are already helping. In fact, an adult probably gave you this book to read.

How to Use This Book

Start by choosing **one** asset to add. Read the stories at the beginning and end of that chapter. The stories are examples of the assets in everyday life. Then pick **one** idea and try it. See how it goes. After that, try another idea, or move on to another asset.

Don't worry about being perfect or getting it right. Know that by trying, you're doing something great for yourself.

The more assets you add, the better you'll feel about yourself and your future. Soon you won't be a kid anymore. You'll be a teenager. Because you have assets, you'll feel and be a lot more sure of yourself. You'll make better decisions. You'll have a head start on success.

We wish you the very best as you add assets to your life.

Pamela Espeland and Elizabeth Verdick
Minneapolis, MN

A Few Words About Families

Kids today live in many different kinds of families.

Maybe you live with one or both of your parents. Maybe you live with other adult relatives—aunts and uncles, grandparents, grown-up brothers or sisters or cousins.

Maybe you live with a stepparent, foster parent, or guardian. Maybe you live with one of your parents and his or her life partner.

In this series, we use the word **parents** to describe the adults who care for you in your home. We also use **family adults, family grown-ups,** and **adults at home.** When you see any of these words, think of your own family, whatever kind it is.

Achievement Motivation

What it means: You want to do well in school, and you try your best.

Mitchell & Tyler's Story

"Hey, Mitch, check these out," Tyler whispers. He fans out his new baseball cards under his desk, where the teacher can't see.

"Yeah . . . uh, cool," Mitchell says, only half looking. Ms. Kingston is talking about the archaeologist who discovered "Sue," the biggest *Tyrannosaurus rex* ever found. Mitchell doesn't want to miss a word.

"Look at this guy," Tyler continues. "Can you believe his batting average is—"

"Tyler!" Ms. Kingston says. "This is the second time I've caught you talking while I'm talking."

Tyler mumbles an apology and looks down at his desk. Mitchell feels bad for Tyler, but in a way, he's glad Ms. Kingston scolded him. "At least now he might keep quiet!" Mitchell thinks. Then he feels kind of rotten. After all, he and Tyler are best friends.

Ms. Kingston asks the class to write about an imaginary archaeological dig. "Using lots of detail, describe what you find in the sand and rock. Name the dinosaur you discover and what it eats. After you've written at least one page, you can draw a picture of it."

Mitchell pulls out his pencils and markers, then prints a title at the top of his paper: TERRIBLE TYRANNOSAURUS. "I am a famous archaeologist," he writes, "digging in the hot Montana sun. I have small tools like a dentist would use. T-Rex is my 'prey' today . . . ."

Mitchell writes the words fast so he can start drawing. As he chooses a green marker to make the dinosaur's head, he notices that Tyler isn't at his desk. Instead, he's over by his cubby, arranging his baseball cards.

Ms. Kingston notices, too. She walks over to Tyler and says. "I'll need to take those from you now. You can have them back when you finish the assignment."

"But—"

"I need one page from you, Tyler. No excuses. Please sit down and get started."

Tyler flops into his seat and crosses his arms over his chest. "I'm *not* going to do this stupid assignment!" he says to Mitchell hotly.

Tyler doesn't have the *Achievement Motivation* asset, but Mitchell does.

Think about your own life. Do you want to do well in school? Do you try as hard as you can—even when what you're learning is hard, or you don't really care that much about it?

If **YES**, keep reading to learn ways to make this asset even stronger.

If **NO**, keep reading to learn ways to add this asset to your life.

Facts!

Kids with the *Achievement Motivation* asset:

✓ **get better grades in school**

✓ **feel more connected to their school**

✓ **have higher hopes for their own future**

You can also use these ideas to help add this asset for other people—like your friends, family members, neighbors, and kids at school.

ways to Add This Asset

AT HOME

Talk About School. Your family is busy, like most families these days. But there are times when it's important to talk: at the dinner table, during car or bus rides,

and before bed. Why these times? Because *mealtime* is when the whole family is gathered. Because *drive time* means you're sitting close together and can have a good conversation. And because *bedtime* gives you a chance to look back on the day and talk about what might happen tomorrow. During these moments, tell your parents a few of the things you've learned in school. Like, "Math was all about fractions again," or, "My teacher is reading us this really cool book called *A Wrinkle in Time.*" Let your mom or dad know what's going well at school and what could go better.

Share What You Learn. Younger siblings and cousins would probably love it if you'd teach them some of the things you know. Give them a few math tips, show them harder spelling words, help them practice their drawing skills, or teach them your best athletic moves. This lets you brush up on your skills and show off a little.

> **TiP:** If your parents are excited about your schoolwork, be sure to share it with them. Bring home your reports, artwork, quizzes, and tests. If it seems that your parents aren't interested in something you've learned, maybe you can find a neighbor, a teacher, or another caring adult who would love to talk it over with you.

Ask Questions, Find Answers. You're at an age when your mind is brimming with curiosity and questions. *Why did the dinosaurs die out? How big is the universe? Why can't humans fly like birds? What is gravity all about? How come some words—"ache," "through," "people"—are spelled so weird?* You're also at an age when you have more skills to look for answers. You can look in books or online, if you have access to a computer and are allowed to use the Internet. Need someone to point you in the right direction? Ask a parent or other family grown-up.

4 Great Places to Find Answers

Want answers? Here are four tried-and-true places to look. Want help? Ask the media specialist at your school. Or visit the public library in your community and get to know the children's librarian. Most librarians love curious kids and want to help. It's also possible that you have some of these resources at home. Ask your parents if you can use them.

1. Encyclopedias. Some encyclopedias are written especially for kids, like the *Scholastic Children's Encyclopedia*. Depending on your reading skills, you might try the *World Book Encyclopedia* or even the *Encyclopaedia Britannica*. Some encyclopedias are on CD-ROM so you can search them quickly on a computer.

2. Almanacs. Updated every year, *The World Almanac for Kids* is packed with facts and

answers. Another book that's fun to browse: *Guinness World Records*. Look here to find the tallest, shortest, oldest, youngest, biggest, smallest, fastest, slowest . . . .

3. Books of answers. Some books focus on specific topics, like geography, space, and history. Ask a librarian to show you some of the New York Public Library Books for Kids or other "answer books."

4. The Internet. Try one or more of these kid-friendly sites. Type in a question or words to search for.

★ Ask Jeeves for Kids: *www.ajkids.com*

★ KidsClick: *www.kidsclick.org*

★ Yahooligans: *yahooligans.yahoo.com*

P.S. You might have heard the saying, "Knowledge is power." Knowing how and where to find answers to your questions is a powerful feeling.

Look Ahead. You may be in elementary school now, but middle school is right around the corner. If you're already in middle school or junior high, then before long you'll be in high school. Do you think about what it will be like when you're older and going to a different school? Do you think ahead to what college or technical school you might want to go to someday? Do you think you might want to join the military or the Peace Corps? While those days might seem far away, it can be exciting—and motivating—to dream about them. And not only dream about them, but even think of ways to stretch yourself toward that future. *Examples:* Talk to older siblings, cousins, or friends who've been through junior high and high school, and ask what it was like. What would have made the experience better for them? Ask some of the grown-ups in your family about their career paths. Why did they choose the job they're in? What kind of schooling did their career require? With your parents or another caring adult, pick a day when you can go to their job with them to see what they do. You may want to write in your journal about the things you learn.

A message for you

Motivation is the "I want it!" feeling that makes you work hard to do something. People can try to motivate you from the outside—like when Grandma promises you a present if you get a good report card. But the strongest motivation comes from the inside—like when you're so into nailing a move on your skateboard that you practice for hours until you get it. Can you think of a time when you were really motivated to do something? How did it feel? What did you accomplish?

 **AT SCHOOL**

★ Get to know your teachers. Say hi and smile when you walk into the classroom and good-bye when you leave. Say hi and wave when you see them in the hall at school—or in the aisle at the grocery store. Tell them a little about yourself. Ask them how their day is going.

> **TIP:** Teachers are people, too. The more interested you are in them, the more interested they will be in you. This can help you want to succeed in school.

★ Does it sometimes seem like school is a waste of time? Talk with your teachers. Say that you really *want* to do well in school. If something is hard for you to do, tell them about it. ***Examples:*** Is it hard for you to sit still in class? Or read what's on the board? Or listen when someone else is talking? Do you have a tough time writing reports? Teachers may be able to help you solve these problems.

★ Is there a subject that totally stumps you? Talk with your teacher. See if you can get extra help before or after school, or maybe during recess. Ask if there's another student—someone a grade ahead of you, or even a high-school student—who can tutor you.

IN YOUR NEIGHBORHOOD

★ Are there neighbors you look up to and admire? Talk with them about school and learning. What were their favorite subjects? How did they do in school? What motivated them?

★ Set a good example for the younger kids in your neighborhood. Don't talk about school being "dumb" or "boring." If that's how you hear them talking, remind them of how important it is to do well in school.

TIP: If younger kids you know are having trouble with a school subject, offer to help them learn. Listen as they read aloud. Help them practice writing their letters or numbers. Show them some of your own schoolwork. (That might motivate them to get excited about school!)

IN YOUR FAITH COMMUNITY

★ If your family belongs to a faith community, you probably go to religious education classes. You may not get grades or have to take tests, but these classes are important, too. They teach you about your faith, its traditions, its stories, and its beliefs. They teach about peace, justice, and service to others. They build good values and character. Religion classes can make you a better person—and help you make the world a better place. So it's worth paying attention, just like you do in school.

 ## WITH YOUR FRIENDS

★ Do your friends have a bad attitude about school? Do they give you a hard time about wanting to do well? Tell them that you *like* school. Let them know you're going to keep working hard. Maybe you can set a good example for them to follow. You and your friends don't all have to be straight-A students or goody-goody teachers' pets. But you'll be in school for a lot more years. Try to make the most of it.

Start Adding!

Pick at least ONE idea you've read here and give it a try. Then thiNK about or write about what happened. Will you try another way to do better in school and stay motivated to succeed?

Back to
Mitchell
& Tyler's
Story

"Come on, Tyler, you've got to write *something*," Mitchell says. "You want your baseball cards back, don't you?"

Tyler shrugs. "Aw, man, who cares? I can't write anything good. I stink at school."

"No, you don't. Besides, this dinosaur stuff is pretty cool. Wait a sec, I'll get my dinosaur library book from my cubby so you can take a look."

When Mitchell returns, he sets the book on Tyler's desk and says, "Check it out." Tyler rolls his eyes and mumbles, "Whatever." But he begins to flip through the pages. Mitchell goes back to his picture, filling in the T-Rex's huge teeth.

"Whoa," says Tyler. He holds up a picture of *Ankylosaurus,* a spiky-backed dinosaur with a long, knobby tail.

"Yeah, that one could swing its tail like crazy," says Mitchell.

"Kind of like a baseball bat!" Tyler says, smiling.

"Yeah! You could write that down."

Tyler gets some paper and a pencil and begins to do the assignment. After a while, Mitchell hears him snort.

"What's up?" Mitchell asks him.

"It says here that Ankylosaurs were plant-eaters. They had really big guts for digesting rough plants. So, dude, they probably had a lot of gas!"

Both boys start laughing. Tyler says, "Mitch, thanks for the book. You're right, this dinosaur stuff is cool."

Just then, Ms. Kingston comes over to check their work. "That's an awesome Tyrannosaurus drawing, Mitchell," she says. "And Tyler, look at that, you've almost written two pages. I'm impressed."

Tyler smiles at her. "Really? Thanks!"

Ms. Kingston slips him his baseball cards and says, "I knew you could do it."

Learning Engagement

WenDy's Story

Over breakfast, Wendy pages through the new issue of *National Geographic Kids,* looking at the glossy photos. She finds an article on caves and soon gets lost in her thoughts.

"I wonder what it would be like to go through a real cave?" she thinks. "I'd have to bring a bright flashlight and wear a hardhat, too. It would be as dark as the back of my closet—no, darker. How spooky would that be?"

She jumps up from the table and runs to her room. She pulls down the shades, goes inside the closet, and shuts the door. She imagines she hears water drip-drip-dripping from the cave's ceiling and walls. She crawls over the pile of shoes and pretends the clothes touching her head are bats.

Then she hears her mom calling. "Wendy! The bus will be here in ten minutes. Where are you?"

"In here, Mom! I'm spelunking!"

She hears her mom enter the room. "You're what?"

Wendy opens the closet and steps out. "Spelunking. It means I'm exploring a cave."

"Well, that's great, honey, but could you explore it after school? Your cereal's getting soggy, and I don't want you to miss the bus."

Wendy sighs. "Mom, you're spoiling all the fun."

"I'm sorry. Tell you what. After school, you can fill me in on spelunking, or whatever it's called, okay? We can even get some library books on caves, if you'd like."

"I'd like," Wendy answers, giving her mom a quick hug.

Wendy has the *Learning Engagement* asset.

Think about your own life. Do you like to learn new things? Do you pay attention in school and participate in class? Do you have hobbies or other learning activities that you do outside of school?

If **YES**, keep reading to learn ways to make this asset even stronger.

If **NO**, keep reading to learn ways to add this asset to your life.

Facts!

Kids with the *Learning Engagement* asset:

✓ **do better in school**

✓ **score higher on tests**

✓ **have better school attendance**

You can also use these ideas to help add this asset for other people—like your friends, family members, neighbors, and kids at school.

Ways to Add This Asset

 AT HOME

Get a Hobby. Hobbies and activities that you do at home are not only fun, but are also great ways to learn. ***Examples:*** If you're a baseball card collector, you're reading all that information about each player, and probably learning some of it by heart. If you play a musical instrument, you're learning how to read music—something a lot of people can't do. If you're an artist, you're stretching your creativity muscles, which can help you in school. No hobby or activity? Think of one you might want to try. *Ideas:* puzzles, collections (rocks, shells, stickers, anything), a musical instrument, studying the stars and planets, reading, writing poems and stories.

Be a Curious Cat. Curious people ask a lot of questions. Their vocabularies are filled with "Who?" "What?" "Where?" "When?" "Why?" and "How?" They are always learning new things. Who are (or were) some of these people? Benjamin Franklin, Isabel Allende, Thomas Jefferson, Marie Curie, George Washington

Carver, Wilma Mankiller, Albert Einstein, Maya Lin, Bill Gates, Oprah Winfrey, S. I. Hayakawa . . . the list goes on and on. Learn more about them and get inspired. You might check their biographies out of the library or read about them online.

Watch What You Eat. A healthy diet helps you stay focused and pay attention while learning. Now that you're older, you're choosing more of the foods you eat, instead of having a parent or another grown-up do this for you. Maybe you eat a hot lunch at school every day, or you pack your own lunch in the morning. You might make your own breakfast and fix your own snacks. Try to eat at least five servings of fruits and vegetables each day. Does that sound like a lot? Don't worry: Raisins and fruit juice can count toward that five. Limit junk foods (candy, chips, sodas, doughnuts, fries), which have a lot of fat, sugar, and salt. These are fine sometimes, but not for every snack or meal.

Take Care of Your Body and Brain. When it comes to learning, it's important to have a tuned-in brain. You're more likely to tune *out* if you're a couch potato. Experts are talking about how kids today are heavier and less active. What's going on? Partly, it's because kids spend more time watching TV or playing video/computer games instead of exercising. Try to get outside and play after school and as much as you can on weekends. When the weather is yucky or you don't have a place to play, do physical activities indoors. You can dance, do jumping-jacks or push-ups, jump rope, or whatever gets you moving. (Just be sure you've got enough room and aren't crashing into the furniture.) Exercise keeps your body and brain in shape for learning.

Get Some Rest. Did you know that sleep helps you learn and grow? It's true! During sleep, your body is busy doing more growing. At your age, you may need

more than eight hours of sleep each night—more like nine or ten. You may have earned a later bedtime now that you're older, but if you're too tired during the day, go to bed an hour earlier. When you're rested, your brain works better and you're more able to concentrate on school, sports, and activities.

8 Signs That You're Not Getting Enough Sleep . . .

1. You Y-A-W-N a lot.

2. You have a hard time listening at home and at school.

3. You forget what you learned in school.

4. You feel tired most of the time.

5. You're often sad or grumpy.

6. You don't have much energy for sports, games, or chores.

7. You have trouble making good choices.

8. You head for the couch the minute you get home.

... and 8 Ways to Sleep Better (zzzzzzzzz)

1. Have a regular sleep schedule. Go to bed at the same time every night, and get up at the same time every morning.

2. Have a regular bedtime routine. Spend time relaxing. Take a warm bath or shower. Listen to quiet music. Read a book (but not a scary book, or a mystery that keeps you turning the pages).

3. Don't drink sodas with caffeine after lunch (or at all).

4. Try not to watch TV or play video games within one hour of your bedtime.

5. Get some exercise every day. Try not to exercise within three hours of your bedtime.

continued →

6. It's okay to have a snack before bedtime, but not a big, heavy meal. Try a glass of milk (it really works!) or some fruit.

7. Keep your bedroom cool, quiet, and dark at night. If you live in a noisy building or share a room with a snoring sibling, buy some earplugs. If you can't control the amount of light in the room, try a sleep mask.

8. When you get into bed, try to think calm, happy thoughts. Don't think about tomorrow's spelling test or the big game. Worries can keep you awake.

At School

Try to Like It. You'll spend 13 years of your life in school—longer if you go to college or technical school. That can seem like forever or go by in a flash (well, *almost* a flash). A lot depends on you. You can choose to like school. You can even decide to get *excited* about school. Try to find *one* thing to like about every subject, even if you think it's the most boring thing in the world.

Stay Awake. Make sure to get enough sleep at night. Pinch yourself if you start to get drowsy during class. And if you have a choice, sit up front, not in the very back of the room. The front of the class is where you'll find most of the smart kids. They've figured out that sitting near the teacher helps them tune in to learning.

Participate. Don't just sit there. Raise your hand. Speak up. Ask questions if there's something you don't understand. (This is another way to help yourself stay awake.)

TiP: If you're scared to talk in class, try it just once and see what happens. You'll probably feel a little more confident to try it again.

Be Prepared. Keep up with assignments. Turn in your homework on time. If you fall behind, tell your teacher right away and ask for help. Don't wait until your teacher comes to you about late homework. You *can* catch up. And the sooner you do, the better you'll feel about school and learning.

IN YOUR NEIGHBORHOOD

★ Check out learning opportunities in your neighborhood or community. What about movies at the library? Classes at the park, community center, or museum? Ask your parents or other family grown-ups to help you find new places where you can learn. Or maybe there's a neighbor who can teach you how to knit, how to cook, or how to build a birdhouse.

IN YOUR FAITH COMMUNITY

★ If you go to religious education classes, try to like them. Stay awake. Participate. Be prepared. Do these sound like the same ideas listed under "In Your School"? That's because they are. Your faith community is another place where you can learn a lot—if you want to. It's also a great place to find others who share your interests.

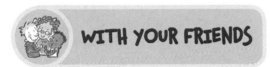 **WITH YOUR FRIENDS**

★ If you hear about a fun class for kids at your community center, invite a friend to sign up with you.

★ Decide together to learn something new. Then find someone to teach you. Ask a parent or another family grown-up for help. ***Examples:*** You might find someone to teach you how to make bread, tune up a bicycle, plant a garden, play the piano, or speak another language. What would *you* like to learn?

★ Challenge each other to get excited and stay excited about school. Talk about your favorite subjects and why you like them so much. Talk about your favorite teachers and what makes them so great. Share things you learn. Encourage each other to do well in school.

Start Adding!

Pick at least ONE idea you've read here and give it a try. Then think about or write about what happened. Will you try another way to make learning more fun and interesting?

Back to
Wendy's
Story
During school, Wendy works on the usual stuff—math, language arts, social studies, and science. She likes all of her subjects, but science and nature are her special interests.

Mr. Chen, her teacher, always lets his students do "independent learning" if they finish their assignments early. And sometimes that includes going to the media center to use the computers.

After Wendy gets done with her spelling list, she brings it to Mr. Chen so he can check it. "Great work!" he says. "Only one error. For homework tonight, you can review that rule about *i* before *e*. Well, now, it looks like you're ready for independent learning."

"Yeah," Wendy answers. "Today I'm really into caves and things that live in the dark."

"Caves, huh? I love caves. They're mysterious."

"Uh-huh. I think I want to learn some stuff about bats."

"Ah," Mr. Chen says. "Do you know about *Stellaluna?*"

"Stella-what?"

Mr. Chen laughs. "It's a great story about a baby bat and how she learns to survive without her mother."

"Okay. What else should I look for?"

"Would you be interested in learning about echolocation? It's how some types of bats find their way in the dark."

"Can you help me spell that?"

He writes the word on a piece of paper and hands it to Wendy. Then he tells her she can go to the media center for one half-hour.

"Thanks!" she says.

As she's walking to the media center, Wendy thinks about Mr. Chen. She loves the way he gets excited about all kinds of different stuff. "Kind of like I do," she thinks.

It feels good to know that she and her teacher have this quality in common.

Homework

What it means: You usually hand in your homework on time.

Kenny & Nina's Story

"This video game is the coolest," Kenny says while eating raisins.

"Don't talk with your mouth full," Nina tells her twin brother.

"You sound like Mom," Kenny replies. Then he opens his mouth wider to gross his sister out.

"Ewwww! Kenny, you're a dork!"

"Takes one to know one," he says, laughing.

They keep playing, each of them rising to new levels in the game. It's fun, and they don't want to stop. But then Dad comes in and sees that the twins haven't budged for the past hour. "Okay, kids," he says. "Time to take a break from the games and get busy on homework."

"Awwww," they groan. But they both go upstairs to their rooms, knowing that Mom and Dad expect the homework to get done without complaint.

On the way, Kenny says to Nina, "If we both finish fast, we'll still have time to get a few more games in before dinner."

"Okay," Nina replies. "But don't start the game without me—promise?"

"I promise. But hurry, okay?"

Kenny spreads his assignments out on his bed. He ignores his math because it's his hardest subject, and decides to fill out the Spanish worksheet instead. "Done!" he announces to his cat, Buster, tossing the paper on his nightstand.

Meanwhile, Nina sits at her desk staring into space. She has already finished her math homework, but isn't sure what to do about the rest—since she accidentally left her Spanish worksheet in her locker.

She hears Kenny knocking at her door. "Can I copy your math?" he asks. "If you let me copy your Spanish worksheet first thing at school tomorrow, so I can still turn mine in on time."

"Deal," Kenny answers. "Let's get back to the game."

Kenny and Nina think they have the *Homework* asset—but there's room for improvement.

Think about your own life. Do you usually do your homework and hand it in on time?

If **YES,** keep reading to learn ways to make this asset even stronger.

If **NO,** keep reading to learn ways to add this asset to your life.

You can also use these ideas to help add this asset for other people—like your friends, family members, neighbors, and kids at school.

Facts!

Kids with the *Homework* asset:

✔ **get better grades in school**

✔ **score higher on tests**

✔ **have fewer behavior problems at school**

Ways to Add This Asset

 **AT HOME**

Beat the Homework Blahs. If you like homework, raise your hand! Hey, your hand's not up. Probably because homework isn't as fun as spending time with friends and family, playing outside, going on the computer, watching movies, relaxing, or working on hobbies. Homework is a "have to"—you have to do it, or you might fall behind in school or get in trouble. Since you can't escape it, you might as well find ways to get it done better, faster, and smarter. That's what the ideas in this chapter are for.

Keep Your Brain Turned On. After a long day at school, it's easy to come home and veg out in front of the TV or computer. That's fine for a half-hour or so (especially if you're watching something about history or nature, or surfing educational Web sites for kids). But too much screen time can drain your brain. Stay tuned in to learning by doing something with your hands. Draw, paint, knit, build, plant, bead, mold with clay—whatever you like. Read a book or write a letter to a friend or relative. Get some fresh air or exercise indoors. It's okay to take a break, but you want to stay sharp for what's next: homework!

Look at Your Homework Habits. Do you do your homework while lying on your bed, blasting music, and watching TV? Do you break for computer games and then forget to finish your math assignment? Do you munch on junk food? If you answered yes to any (or all) of these questions, it's time to change those horrid homework habits. *Examples:* Sit up instead of lying down while you work, so you stay awake and alert. Try healthy snacks like fruit, carrots and celery sticks, raisins, or yogurt. Save the music, TV, and computer games for later. (You might want to use them as rewards for finishing your work.) Here are three more steps you can take toward getting your homework done better, faster, and smarter . . . .

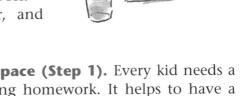

Make Your Own Space (Step 1). Every kid needs a quiet place for doing homework. It helps to have a desk, a comfortable chair, and good lighting. Why? Simple: so you can sit upright, spread out your work, and see what you're doing. If you're lucky enough to have a desk in your bedroom, go take a look at it. Is it neat and tidy . . . or a total mess? Are supplies like extra paper, pencils, and a calculator handy . . . or somewhere, but you're not sure where? Getting organized is one of the keys to school success. You'll feel better knowing that you have your own personal workspace, where you can find what you need when you need it.

TIP: If you don't have a desk, ask your dad or mom if you can get one. Thrift shops and garage sales are good places to look for affordable used furniture. Or you could set up a study space with a lamp at a table.

How to Avoid a Desk-Sharing Disaster

Maybe you share a desk with a sibling. What if one of you is neat and the other is a slob? What if one of you uses all the staples and tape but never refills them? Or leaves sticky fingerprints and crumbs all over the computer keyboard?

Have a family meeting to talk about fair ways to share space. Maybe your family could make a homework schedule so you always know whose turn it is to use the desk. *P.S.* A homework schedule is an excellent thing, whether you share a desk or not. See **Make a Plan (Step 3).**

Get Organized (Step 2). Once you've got a neat, orderly desk, it's time for the next step: organizing *yourself.* Start by taking a good look at your backpack. What's in there? Folded-up, wadded-up, crumpled-up papers? Broken pencils? Old bubblegum? That's not a backpack, it's a bad dream. An organized backpack includes these things: the books you need for school and homework; folders and notebooks for each subject (your teacher can help you figure out what you need); and a pencil box or pouch for writing supplies, erasers, a calculator, and other small items that can get lost. Try to form new backpack habits. Each morning before you leave home, check to see that you've got what you need: finished homework, signed permission slips, freshly sharpened pencils. Each afternoon at school, check again. Did you pack your assignments, notes, textbooks, school supplies, library card, and so on? Don't leave school without them!

Make a Plan (Step 3). Have you noticed that some adults carry their day planner, mini-calendar, or hand-held computer everywhere they go? Or that they're always making to-do lists? Busy people—whether grown-ups or kids—need tools and a plan to get things done. Maybe you already have a planner for school. If not, ask your parents to help you get a kid-sized day planner so you can keep track of your activities and assignments. (Or make a monthly or weekly calendar by hand or on a computer.) At the start of each week, write down your after-school plans like sports, lessons, play dates, and worship activities. Then figure out where your homework time fits in by making a homework schedule. Is it possible to do your work right after dinner each night? Can you get a whole hour of un-interrupted time, or do you need to break it up into half-hour slots? A family adult or your teacher can help you come up with a homework schedule that works for you.

Do Your Own Work . . . But Get Help If You Need It. There are two homework pitfalls you may know about: (1) copying someone else's homework, and (2) getting Mom or Dad to do the work for you. If you and your friends are into copying, ask yourself why. Are you bored? Do you not understand the work? Are you feeling lazy? Confused? Is there not enough time to get it all done? Copying someone else's work is a short-term solution—plus it's cheating. If you get away with it, you may receive credit for doing the work, but you haven't actually learned anything. Sooner or later, that's going to cause problems. (For example, when it's test time, you might not know the answers.) Getting a parent to help you with homework is fine—but not if Mom or Dad is mostly doing the work for you. Again, you're not really learning. If you're having a lot of trouble starting your work, understanding it, or finishing it, talk to a grown-up at home or school. You might say, "I'm having a hard time with my homework. Can you help me figure out why and what to do?"

 **AT SCHOOL**

★ Each day before you leave school, make sure that you understand the homework for that day. Did you copy down the assignments? Do you have the worksheets and handouts? What about the books? Do you know for sure when things are due? What about long-term projects? Take a moment at your desk or your locker to think through what you need.

★ If you have free time during the school day, why not use it for homework? Maybe your bus arrives a half-hour before school starts, or leaves a half-hour after school ends. Is there somewhere you can go to work?

> **TiP:** This doesn't mean waiting until the morning to *start* your homework. (What if it takes longer?) Instead, you might use that time to review a list of spelling words, or check the work you did the night before.

★ If all or most of your homework seems dull and boring, talk with your teacher. See if you can do other types of assignments that are more interesting for you.

★ If you feel that you're getting too much homework, or you don't understand the homework, talk with your teacher. That's what teachers are for!

A message for you

Homework doesn't exist just to make your life miserable. It's a tool for learning new skills and practicing them until you've totally got them down. Think of homework as swimming laps in a pool. You don't expect laps to be tons of fun, but you know you have to do them to get stronger and be a better swimmer. All that (home)work pays off.

 ## IN YOUR NEIGHBORHOOD

★ Do you need some one-on-one homework help? Maybe there's a willing teenager who lives on your block or in your building. With your parents or other family grown-ups, ask around. Or maybe you can be a homework helper for a younger kid in your neighborhood.

IN YOUR FAITH COMMUNITY

★ Talk about homework with your religion class or youth group. Find connections between your faith and doing your homework. *Example:* You could link homework to positive values like responsibility, honesty, and respect.

WITH YOUR FRIENDS

★ Start a study group—but only if you really plan to study. Make a list of people you might want to

study with. Keep it small—three or four kids at the most. Then try it at your house, or a friend's house. Or maybe you could meet at the local library, your community center, or your place of worship.

Start Adding!

Pick at least ONE idea you've read here and give it a try. Then think about or write about what happened. Will you try another way to get your homework done and hand it in on time?

Back to Kenny & Nina's Story

During dinner, Mom asks the twins, "Homework done?"

"Pretty much," Nina answers.

"Well, good. Dad and I are proud of you both."

Kenny's eyes meet Nina's, then they both look away. Nina stands up quickly and says, "Mom, I'll help you with the dishes."

"Thanks, hon," she replies.

"Kenny," says Dad, "can you help me with some stuff in the garage?"

"Sure. I'll go upstairs and get a sweatshirt."

Moments later Mom, Dad, and Nina hear a loud "Oh nooooo!" from upstairs. Kenny comes running into the kitchen. "Look what Buster did!" He holds up his soggy Spanish worksheet. "He knocked over a water glass on my nightstand, and now my homework is ruined!"

"Oh noooooo," moans Nina. "What am I going to do?"

"What do you mean, what are *you* going to do?" Dad asks Nina. "It's Kenny's homework, not yours."

Nina freezes. "Um, right. I mean, I was just feeling bad for Kenny."

"What's going on here?" Mom asks. She looks first at Nina, then at Kenny. Neither one looks back at her.

Kenny puts his homework on the table and begins to wipe it off with some napkins. The paper smears and then tears. "Darn cat," he mutters.

Dad crosses his arms and says, "We're waiting." Nina looks down at her feet.

"I guess we'd better tell them," says Kenny.

"We've been copying each other's homework," Nina admits.

"How long has this been going on?" Mom asks. Nina and Kenny both shrug.

"A while?" asks Dad.

"Yeah," they both say.

"Okay," Dad sighs. "That's it for the video games until we get into some better routines around here."

"Yep, he's right," Mom agrees. "And the four of us are going to sit down and have a long talk about homework rules, honesty, and cheating."

Nina asks quietly, "Are you guys really mad at us?"

"We're disappointed in what you've done," Dad answers.

Buster slinks into the kitchen and rubs his fur against Kenny's legs. Kenny picks him up, and Nina comes over and scratches under the cat's chin.

"But we'll forgive you," Mom says. "Just like you two forgive Buster."

Bonding to Adults at School

What it means: You care about and feel connected to the teachers and other adults at your school.

T. J.'s Story

"Yum," T. J. says. "This spaghetti is the best, Dad."

"Thanks, T. J. I'm glad you like my special sauce. Can you pass me some garlic bread, please?"

"Sure. Oh, Dad, I just remembered about the field trip to the nature center next week. I have the permission slip in my backpack."

"Okay, I'll sign it. How are things going in Mr. Hoffman's class?"

"Pretty good," T. J. replies.

"Just pretty good?"

"Well, yeah, he helps me out when I get overloaded. He lets me go take a break outside the classroom and stuff. And I think the field trip will be fun."

"Are you feeling like you fit in with the other kids?" his dad asks.

"I guess."

"You don't sound so sure. Do you feel like special ed was more right for you? We can always change our minds if the regular class isn't working out."

"Nah. It's not that, Dad. I just miss my old teacher. Mrs. Levitz was always there for me, you know? She didn't have as many kids in her room, so her class was kind of like . . . more like a family. That sounds dumb, right?"

"It doesn't sound dumb at all."

T. J. asks for more sauce. While passing the bowl, his dad says, "T. J., I have an idea."

"What?"

"Let's invite Mrs. Levitz over for dinner."

T. J. chokes a little on his milk. "You mean *here?*"

"Sure. Why not?" his dad asks.

"Do you think she'd come?"

"Only if we ask."

T. J. laughs. "Okay!"

T. J. and his dad want to make sure the *Bonding to Adults at School* asset is part of T. J.'s life.

Think about your own life. Do you care about your teacher (or teachers, if you have more than one)? How about other adults at school, like the teachers' aides, your principal, the school counselor, and the people who work in the office? Do you feel close and connected to some of these people? That's what *bonding* is all about.

> **Facts!**
>
> **Kids with the *Bonding to Adults at School* asset:**
>
> ✓ **are happier in school**
>
> ✓ **feel more motivated to learn**
>
> ✓ **are less *aggressive* (pushy and violent)**

If **YES,** keep reading to learn ways to make this asset even stronger.

If **NO,** keep reading to learn ways to add this asset to your life.

You can also use these ideas to help add this asset for other people—like your friends, family members, neighbors, and kids at school.

ways to Add This Asset

At Home

Tell Your Family About the Adults at Your School. Your dad and mom probably know the name of your teacher, and may have met him or her at school conferences, parents' night, or school events. But how well do your parents know the principal, teachers' aides, administrators, lunch servers, media center staff, school counselor, gym teachers and coaches, custodians, bus drivers, and . . . ? (The list goes on and on!) There are many adults who keep your school running, and all of them are important. So, when you're talking with your family about school, mention these people by name—if you know their names. If you don't know their names or who they are, that's what this asset is all about.

Remember Special Days. There are a few times each year when you might want to give your teacher something special: before the winter holidays, on her or his birthday, and on the last day of school. You can ask a family grown-up to take you shopping for a small, inexpensive gift. Even better, you can make one at home with your own art supplies. You don't need to impress your teacher with something fancy. Sometimes, a kind and heartfelt note that says, "You're a great teacher!" is the best present a teacher can receive. You could ask the grown-ups in your family to sign the note or write one of their own. *P.S.* Notes like these can be for any time of the year, not just special times.

Get Your Family Involved. Make a list of the adults at school who know the kids well and show they care about them. In what ways do they show it? *Examples:* Maybe your bus driver greets every student by name each morning and afternoon. Or your coach finds ways to give every team member a

> **TIP:** You might see if your mom or dad would like to get more involved with the adults at your school. How about becoming a parent volunteer? Or a member of the PTO or PTA? Or going to more school conferences, events, and meetings?

chance to play instead of sitting on the sidelines. Or your teacher has a way of inspiring students to work hard and do their best. Take your list to a family grown-up, then ask that person to help you think of ways you and your family can thank these people.

Invite Your Teacher to Dinner. This may sound weird, but many students and their families do it (and not to get better grades!). Inviting your teacher to your home for a meal is a nice way for everyone to get to know each other better. It's fun to see your teacher somewhere besides standing in front of the blackboard. You could learn things you never knew about your teacher's family, pets, hobbies, and life outside of school.

How to Invite Your Teacher to Dinner

1. Ask your parents if it's okay to invite your teacher to dinner. Pick a day and time that works for everyone.

2. Write out an invitation for your teacher. This way, you won't forget any of the important details. You can write it by hand, write it on a computer and print it out, or buy an invitation card at a store (these have

blanks for you to fill in). Your invitation
might look like this:

> ## You're invited to dinner!
>
> *To:* <u>Mr. Shadid</u>
>
> *From:* <u>Alicia Watson and her parents, Tom and</u>
> <u>Miranda Watson</u>
>
> *When:* <u>7:00 P.M., Friday, February 18</u>
>
> *Where:* <u>Our place: 359 North Waverly Street,</u>
> <u>Apartment 8-B (call if you need directions)</u>
>
> *Bring:* <u>Yourself!</u>
>
> *Please call to let us know if you can come:*
> 555-2345

3. Give your teacher the invitation.

4. When your teacher calls to accept your
   invitation, this would be a good time for
   you (or your parents) to ask if there's anything he or she can't eat or doesn't like to
   eat. Some people have allergies to things
   like milk or peanuts. Some people are veg-
   etarians who don't eat meat. Some people
   can't eat seafood. It's good to know this
   ahead of time, so your teacher can actually
   eat what you serve.

AT SCHOOL

Be Friendly. Give the adults at your school a smile, a wave, and a hello when you see them in the halls, in the cafeteria, or on the bus. They'll appreciate it—and remember you.

Get Involved. Check out what's available at your school. Art club? Spanish or math club? Service clubs? After-school sports? Chances are that all (or most) are led by teachers. Because these groups tend to be smaller than school classes, it's even easier to get to know the grown-ups in charge.

Show Interest. Talk with your teachers before school, after school, or whenever it seems like a good time. How can you start conversations? Easy. Ask them questions about their interests. **_Examples:_** "What did you think of the game on Sunday?" "Have you seen the new _Harry Potter_ movie?" "I saw a picture of a sailboat on your desk. Do you like to go sailing?"

> **TiP:** When you ask people about themselves, this makes _you_ seem more interesting to them.

Be a Good Listener. Listening isn't all about the _ears_. To really show you're listening, look people in the eye when they're talking. Smile and nod your head. Try not to interrupt, even if there's something you can't wait to say back.

IN YOUR NEIGHBORHOOD

★ When you talk with younger kids in your neighborhood, ask them to tell you about school and their teachers. If they don't seem to know their teachers very well, give them a few hints on what to do. Share ideas that have worked for you—like saying hi and smiling.

IN YOUR FAITH COMMUNITY

★ Your religious leaders are also your teachers. Bonding with your religious leaders will make you feel more connected to your faith community. You can use many of the ideas in this chapter to get to know your religious leaders better.

> **TIP:** Sunday-school teachers eat dinner, too! So do priests, pastors, ministers, rabbis, imams, and nuns.

WITH YOUR FRIENDS

★ Invite a favorite teacher to eat lunch with you in the school cafeteria.

★ Volunteer to stay after school to help clean up the classroom. Give up a recess now and then to help a teacher prepare for a lesson.

★ Make a pact with your friends at school to be friendly and respectful to all adults. Set a good example for others to follow.

Start Adding!

Pick at least ONE idea you've read here and give it a try. Then think about or write about what happened. Will you try another way to get to know your teachers and other adults at your school? How will you show that you care?

Back to T. J.'s Story It's Friday night, and T. J. keeps peeking out the window to watch for Mrs. Levitz's car. When she pulls up, T. J. hurries to open the front door. His dad is right behind him.

"Well, hello there!" says Mrs. Levitz with a smile.

"Hi, Carla," says T. J.'s dad. "Nice to see you again."

"Please come in," T. J. adds, remembering to use his best manners.

They all sit in the living room, and T. J.'s dad sets out some crackers and dip.

"I think you'll like what we're having for dinner, Mrs. Levitz," T. J. says. "I got to pick the menu myself!"

"Oh, really?" she answers. "Well, what's on the menu for tonight, my friend?"

"Make-your-own mini-pizzas. You get to choose

what you want: pepperoni, Canadian bacon, olives—anything! Oh, yeah, and salad—Dad says we need some 'roughage,' too. And for dessert, chocolate cake."

"Well, that sounds like a creative and balanced meal," Mrs. Levitz replies.

"I hope you brought your appetite," says T. J.'s dad. "Now, if you two will excuse me for a moment, I'm going to put that salad together and organize our pizza ingredients."

After he leaves the room, Mrs. Levitz turns to T. J. "We sure miss you in class. You always were my best joke-teller. How are things going for you this year?"

"So far, so good. I think."

"Mr. Hoffman has told me some nice things about you," Mrs. Levitz continues. "I hear you're working very hard on making new friends. And he told me your reading skills are getting better every day. I'm proud of you."

T. J. smiles. "Thanks," he says quietly. "Did Mr. Hoffman really tell you that?"

"Of course! Why wouldn't he?"

"I didn't know he noticed that stuff."

"Oh—he notices, all right."

T. J. thinks about this for a while. Then he says, "Maybe I should try out one of my jokes on him sometime."

"Good idea, T. J."

Reading for Pleasure

The Rockin' Readers' Story

"Excellent!" says Janelle as she looks at the snack table. "Nice animal theme, Tim."

Tim smiles. "Yeah, get it? Animal crackers, fish-shaped crackers, and milk—from a cow, you know. I thought it would go along with the book in a weird sort of way."

Katie, the leader for this month's meeting of the Rockin' Readers Club, announces, "Okay, we're all here. Let's get started!"

The eight book club members plop down in comfy chairs or sprawl out on the floor in Tim's rec room. They each have a copy of *Love That Dog* by award-winning author Sharon Creech.

"Katie, this is one of the saddest books I've ever read! Why'd you choose it? Did you want to make us all bawl our eyes out or something?" says Alberto.

"I know, I know," Katie replies. "It's different—I wanted to be different. We've done the Harry Potter thing, and Lemony Snicket. But this book, well, it's a story told in poetry."

"I liked it because it was short!" says Kenny. His twin sister, Nina, rolls her eyes. "Kenny only likes a book if he can finish it in, like, an hour," she says.

"No, seriously," says Kenny. "It's neat how the story says so much in so few words."

"I agree with that," Isabelle adds. "Some pages have only a few lines. But those lines leave you curious—and sad."

"Look at this, everybody!" Maya chimes in. She holds up a photo of her dog, Libby, wearing a silly hat. The other kids pass the photo around, laughing.

"I think maybe Jack's dog, Sky, in the story looked like Libby," Maya says.

"Oh no! I'm feeling sad just thinking about it!" Janelle moans, covering her face. "I love the book, but—oh, can someone please pass me the tissues?!"

"Whoa," says Katie. "I knew this book would be an interesting choice!"

The eight members of the Rockin' Readers Club all have the *Reading for Pleasure* asset.

Think about your own life. Do you read for fun and to learn new things? Do you read something every day—whether that means books, poems, magazines, comic books, song lyrics, riddles, or the newspaper?

If **YES**, keep reading to learn ways to make this asset even stronger.

If **NO**, keep reading to learn ways to add this asset to your life.

> ## Facts!
>
> **Kids with the *Reading for Pleasure* asset:**
>
> ✓ **score higher on achievement tests**
>
> ✓ **are better readers**
>
> ✓ **enjoy reading more**

You can also use these ideas to help add this asset for other people—like your friends, family members, neighbors, and kids at school.

ways to Add This Asset

 **AT HOME**

Head to the Library. If your family doesn't have the library habit, talk to your dad or mom about going more often. Some families like to go as much as every

week or twice a month. The great thing about libraries is that everything is FREE. And you've got a ton of
books, magazines, books on tape and CD, videotapes,
DVDs, music CDs, and more to choose from. Many
libraries have special sections for little kids, teens, and
everyone in between. There may be computers you
can use to browse the Internet and play games. If you
go, plan to stay a while. Spend time in sections you
haven't looked through before. You may find interesting books about famous paintings,
amazing automobiles, mysterious
rainforests, and places around the
world that you can dream of
visiting. Go look at the library's
bulletin board, too—you may see
notices for children's book clubs
or other fun events.

TiP: If your
parents work
during library
hours, ask if
they know other
adults who
could take you.

Get to Know the Librarians. They know a lot about books and authors. They became librarians because (duh) they're really into books. You could go up to a librarian and say, "I'm looking for a mystery that has ghosts in it," or, "I like poems that are funny," and he or she could help you find books that fit either description. If you get to know some of the librarians, they'll get to know you and what kinds of books you like. That will make it even easier for them to help you each time you come in. *P.S.* Librarians are also there for you when you need help researching a topic for a school report or project—or with the basics of how to find things in a library.

Let People Read to You. No matter how old you are, you're never too old to be read to. Think it's not true? Look at all the adults out there who listen to books on tape or CD! Hearing a story told aloud lets your ears, not your eyes, do the work. You can lie back, close your eyes, and relax as the story takes you away. If your dad or mom offers to read to you, say yes. Or why not just ask a family adult to read to you? Say, "Grandpa, can we read this book on whales together?" You can also sit with the grown-ups in your family while they read news magazines or the paper. Ask if they can help you understand some of the articles, too.

Make a Reading Corner. It's such a peaceful feeling when you have a quiet, private place to read books, poems, magazines, and comics. Where do you like to go when you read? Your bed, a comfy couch, a homemade fort, the library, a beanbag chair, the low branch of a big tree, a window seat? Maybe you like to pull the covers over your head at night and read by flashlight. Anything goes. The important thing is to read, *read*, READ!

> **TiP:** While you're reading, you'll come across many new words. Take the opportunity to learn them instead of skipping over them. Ask a family grown-up how to pronounce each word and what it means. Look it up in a dictionary, too. If you'd like, keep a written list of the new words you've learned, with their definitions. You'll probably see the words again when you read, and in case you've forgotten their meaning, you'll have a quick and handy way to look them up. *Bonus:* This will help you do better in spelling and language arts at school.

Keep a Reading Journal. Write down the titles and authors of all the books you read. Write a brief description of each book (don't worry, this isn't a book report!) and what you thought of it. Did you like it? Why or why not? Some people have many years' worth of reading journals. They enjoy looking back and remembering books they read when they were children. Each book is an old friend.

PSSSSSST . . . .

Not everyone is a good reader, okay? Maybe you're reading this book mostly because someone (a teacher or a parent) is making you read it. Maybe you have trouble understanding the words you read, focusing your eyes, or following the words on a page. There may be times when words look backwards or seem to be jumping around. Or perhaps reading leaves you tired and makes your brain hurt. Your parents and teachers may already know that you have a problem with reading, but if they don't, *please tell them.* Getting help for this problem is one of the most important things you'll ever do. If you improve your reading, you'll do better on tests and learn more in and out of school. There are many benefits to becoming a better reader.

AT SCHOOL

★ If you have free time at school, spend it reading—before the day starts or while you're waiting for your bus, during lunch or times when you finish your work before the rest of the class. Always carry a book in your backpack or keep one in your desk or locker.

★ Does your school have a reading club? If it does, think about joining. If it doesn't, what about starting one? Talk with a teacher about how to do this.

★ Volunteer to read aloud to younger kids during lunch or recess.

★ Ask your teacher to tell you about books he or she enjoyed at your age. You might want to read some of them, too. Then you can talk with your teacher about them. ***Bonus:*** This may help you add the *Bonding to Adults at School* asset to your life. See pages 53–65.

IN YOUR NEIGHBORHOOD

★ Depending on where you live, you may have a children's bookstore you can go to. If you do, you're lucky. The store will probably have story times for kids of different ages, book signings with children's authors, and book clubs for young people to join. Some children's bookstores send out newsletters (by mail or email) with news about upcoming events.

★ If you don't have a store made for kids nearby, there may be a general bookstore that carries children's books and has authors come in to read their work or do signings. Some bookstores even have a music café where you can listen to live music or sip hot chocolate while you read.

IN YOUR FAITH COMMUNITY

★ Does your house of worship have a library? Many do. If yours does, check it out. Are there books for kids and teens? Are there comfy chairs to curl up in? If there's no library, talk with adults about starting one. It doesn't have to be a big deal—even a bookcase in the office would be a good start. Adults in your faith community could donate books for kids or teens, or donate money to buy books.

WITH YOUR FRIENDS

★ Challenge each other to read for fun. Talk about books you like. Dress up like your favorite characters. Act out scenes from the stories you've read.

★ When you hear about a movie based on a kids' book, read the book first, go to the movie together, then talk afterward about which you liked better and why—the book or the movie.

★ Share books with each other. When you loan a book to a friend, you might want to write down the names of the book and the borrower so you don't forget to get it back. Or you can make or buy special stickers (called *book plates*) to write your name on and glue inside the front cover.

Ti℘: Sharing books with friends is fun for a lot of reasons. You have someone to talk to about the story afterward. You can have conversations about the characters you loved or hated, what your favorite part was, what you thought of the ending, and which character you'd most want to be.

★ When you borrow a book from a friend (or a family member, or the library), be sure to take good care of it. Don't get messy fingerprints on it, wrinkle the pages, or leave it lying flat (the book's spine can bend and break). Use a bookmark instead of folding down the corner of the page you stopped on. Last but not least, return the book on time.

Start Adding!

Pick at least ONE idea you've read here and give it a try. Then think about or write about what happened. Will you try another way to make reading a bigger part of your life?

Back to the Rockin' Readers' Story

"You know what, you guys?" Alberto asks the group. "The best thing for me about *Love That Dog* was I learned about Walter Dean Myers. He is SO my hero now!"

"What did you learn about him?" Isabelle asks.

"I went on the Internet and looked him up. He's a famous author who's written tons of books and poems and won a bunch of awards. He really does visit schools and talk to kids—just like in the book about Jack and Sky."

"Yeah," Tim says. "I've heard of him 'cause my older sister read a book called *Monster*, which he wrote. I guess his stuff is pretty . . . heavy. I don't know what other word to use."

"He had a tough time while growing up," Alberto continues. "He was raised by a foster family in Harlem, in New York City. The amazing thing is, he had all these behavior troubles in school, but he turned out okay. He had a big problem with speech—he couldn't pronounce words in a way people could understand. But he says one thing saved him: reading."

"That's pretty cool," says Katie. "I think a lot of kids who grow up reading books secretly want to be writers."

"I want to be just like Walter Dean Myers," Alberto admits.

"Well, I want to be J. K. Rowling," says Tim.

"Are you saying you want to be a girl?" Kenny asks, laughing.

"Ha, ha, very funny," Tim answers. "No, I just want to write bestsellers—and be a billionaire."

Nina laughs and says, "Well, someday we can be *your* fan club, then!"

A NOTE TO GROWN-UPS

Ongoing research by Search Institute, a nonprofit organization based in Minneapolis, Minnesota, shows that young people who succeed have specific assets in their lives— **Developmental Assets** including family support, a caring neighborhood, integrity, resistance skills, self-esteem, and a sense of purpose. This book, along with the other seven books in the **Adding Assets Series for Kids,** empowers young people ages 8–12 to build their own Developmental Assets.

But it's very important to acknowledge that building assets for and with young people is primarily an *adult* responsibility. What kids need most in their lives are grown-ups—parents and other relatives, teachers, school administrators, neighbors, youth leaders, religious leaders, community members, policy makers, advocates, and more—who care about them as individuals. They need adults who care enough to learn their names, to show interest in their lives, to listen when they talk, to provide them with opportunities to realize their potential, to teach them well, to give them sound advice, to serve as good examples, to guide them, to inspire them, to support them when they stumble, and to shield them from harm –as much as is humanly possible these days.

This book focuses on five of the 40 Developmental Assets identified by Search Institute. These are **Internal Assets**—values, skills, and self-perceptions that kids develop *internally,* with your help. The five internal assets described here are called the **Commitment to Learning Assets.** They're about taking every opportunity to learn, both in and out of school. Being open to learning new things—and developing the skills needed to learn them—are vital to a child's success, now and in the future.

Every time we adults come in contact with children, we teach them something, whether we know it or not. We're curious—or closed-minded. We're accepting of differences—or judgmental. We communicate that learning is exciting and enjoyable—or that it's drudgery, something to be done only when absolutely necessary. We overemphasize the importance of grades—or stress that what matters most is getting an education. We spend time reading—or we don't. The best example a child can have is a parent or grandparent, aunt or uncle, or other family grown-up who's a passionate lifelong learner.

A list of all 40 Developmental Assets for middle childhood, with definitions, follows. If you want to know more about the assets, some of the resources listed on pages 87–88 will help you. Or you can visit the Search Institute Web site at *www.search-institute.org*.

Thank you for caring enough about kids to make this book available to the young person or persons in your life. We'd love to hear your success stories, and we welcome your suggestions for adding assets to kids' lives—or improving future editions of this book.

Pamela Espeland and Elizabeth Verdick
Free Spirit Publishing Inc.
217 Fifth Avenue North, Suite 200
Minneapolis, MN 55401-1299
help4kids@freespirit.com

The 40 Developmental Assets for Middle Childhood

EXTERNAL ASSETS

SUPPORT

1. **Family support**—Family life provides high levels of love and support.
2. **Positive family communication**—Parent(s) and child communicate positively. Child feels comfortable seeking advice and counsel from parent(s).
3. **Other adult relationships**—Child receives support from adults other than her or his parent(s).
4. **Caring neighborhood**—Child experiences caring neighbors.
5. **Caring school climate**—Relationships with teachers and peers provide a caring, encouraging school environment.
6. **Parent involvement in schooling**—Parent(s) are actively involved in helping the child succeed in school.

EMPOWERMENT

7. **Community values children**—Child feels valued and appreciated by adults in the community.
8. **Children as resources**—Child is included in decisions at home and in the community.
9. **Service to others**—Child has opportunities to help others in the community.
10. **Safety**—Child feels safe at home, at school, and in her or his neighborhood.

BOUNDARIES AND EXPECTATIONS

11. **Family boundaries**—Family has clear and consistent rules and consequences and monitors the child's whereabouts.
12. **School boundaries**—School provides clear rules and consequences.
13. **Neighborhood boundaries**—Neighbors take responsibility for monitoring the child's behavior.
14. **Adult role models**—Parents(s) and other adults in the child's family, as well as nonfamily adults, model positive, responsible behavior.
15. **Positive peer influence**—Child's closest friends model positive, responsible behavior.
16. **High expectations**—Parent(s) and teachers expect the child to do her or his best at school and in other activities.

CONSTRUCTIVE USE OF TIME

17. **Creative activities**—Child participates in music, art, drama, or creative writing two or more times per week.
18. **Child programs**—Child participates two or more times per week in cocurricular school activities or structured community programs for children.
19. **Religious community**—Child attends religious programs or services one or more times per week.
20. **Time at home**—Child spends some time most days both in high-quality interaction with parent(s) and doing things at home other than watching TV or playing video games.

COMMITMENT TO LEARNING

21. **Achievement motivation**—Child is motivated and strives to do well in school.
22. **Learning engagement**—Child is responsive, attentive, and actively engaged in learning at school and enjoys participating in learning activities outside of school.
23. **Homework**—Child usually hands in homework on time.
24. **Bonding to adults at school**—Child cares about teachers and other adults at school.
25. **Reading for pleasure**—Child enjoys and engages in reading for fun most days of the week.

POSITIVE VALUES

26. **Caring**—Parent(s) tell the child it is important to help other people.
27. **Equality and social justice**—Parent(s) tell the child it is important to speak up for equal rights for all people.
28. **Integrity**—Parent(s) tell the child it is important to stand up for one's beliefs.
29. **Honesty**—Parent(s) tell the child it is important to tell the truth.
30. **Responsibility**—Parent(s) tell the child it is important to accept personal responsibility for behavior.
31. **Healthy lifestyle**—Parent(s) tell the child it is important to have good health habits and an understanding of healthy sexuality.

SOCIAL COMPETENCIES

32. **Planning and decision making**—Child thinks about decisions and is usually happy with the results of her or his decisions.
33. **Interpersonal competence**—Child cares about and is affected by other people's feelings, enjoys making friends, and, when frustrated or angry, tries to calm herself or himself.
34. **Cultural competence**—Child knows and is comfortable with people of different racial, ethnic, and cultural backgrounds and with her or his own cultural identity.
35. **Resistance skills**—Child can stay away from people who are likely to get her or him in trouble and is able to say no to doing wrong or dangerous things.
36. **Peaceful conflict resolution**—Child attempts to resolve conflict nonviolently.

POSITIVE IDENTITY

37. **Personal power**—Child feels he or she has some influence over things that happen in her or his life.
38. **Self-esteem**—Child likes and is proud to be the person he or she is.
39. **Sense of purpose**—Child sometimes thinks about what life means and whether there is a purpose for her or his life.
40. **Positive view of personal future**—Child is optimistic about her or his personal future.

Helpful Resources

Books

Help! My Teacher Hates Me: A School Survival Guide for Kids 10 to 14 Years Old by Meg F. Schneider (New York: Workman Publishing, 1994). Solutions and strategies for dealing with the problems and issues every student faces in school, from friends and cheating to homework, extracurricular activities, and actual physical fears.

Reaching Your Goals by Robin Landew Silverman (New York: Franklin Watts, 2004). To turn a wish into a goal takes creative thinking and organized planning skills. This book shows how to make a plan and see it through to the end.

School Smarts: All the Right Answers to Homework, Teachers, Popularity, and More! by Brooks Whitney (Middleton, WI: Pleasant Co. Publications, 2000). Advice on a variety of school-related topics, including getting along with teachers, doing homework, studying for tests, preparing presentations, being popular, and more.

You're Smarter Than You Think: A Kid's Guide to Multiple Intelligences by Thomas Armstrong, Ph.D. (Minneapolis: Free Spirit Publishing, 2001). Being smart means more than getting good grades and test scores in school. Discover eight different ways to be smart, find out which ones you have (hint: all eight!), and learn to strengthen your smarts.

Web sites

B. J. Pinchbeck's Homework Helper
school.discovery.com/homeworkhelp/bjpinchbeck
Hundreds of links to homework help. This site was started by B. J. Pinchbeck ("Beege") and his father in 1996, when Beege was nine years old. More than 10,000 people visit each day.

Class Brain
www.classbrain.com
Brain games, word puzzles, homework help, and creative project ideas. There's also an action adventure arcade and strategy tips for different board and card games.

Fun Brain
www.funbrain.com
Lots of games organized by grade (K–12). Categories include Math Baseball, Funbrain Arcade, Grammar Gorillas, Dare to be Square, and more. Also searchable by subject: Geography, Art, Languages, Math, Music, Science, and Technology.

Yahooligans! Reference
www.yahooligans.yahoo.com/reference
Quick look-ups for all kinds of things you may need (or want) to know, from the capital of Bulgaria to the definition of *synthesis*. Search dictionaries, an encyclopedia, a world factbook, a kids' almanac, a thesaurus, and more.

FOR ADULTS

Books

Building Assets Is Elementary: Group Activities for Helping Kids Ages 8–12 Succeed by Search Institute (Minneapolis: Search Institute, 2004). Promoting creativity, time-management skills, kindness, manners, and more, this flexible activity book includes over 50 easy-to-use group exercises for the classroom or youth group.

Great Books for Girls: More Than 600 Books to Inspire Today's Girls and Tomorrow's Women and *Great Books for Boys:* More than 600 Books for Boys 2 to 14 by Kathleen Odean (New York: Ballantine, 2002 and 1998). Annotated recommendations from a former Caldecott and Newbery Award committee member.

How to Parent So Children Will Learn by Sylvia B. Rimm, Ph.D. (Three Rivers, MI: Three Rivers Press, 1997). Advice on setting limits, selecting appropriate rewards and punishments, decreasing arguments and power struggles, encouraging appropriate independence, guiding children toward good study habits, helping them improve their test-taking skills, and more.

What Kids Need to Succeed: Proven, Practical Ways to Raise Good Kids by Peter L. Benson, Ph.D., Judy Galbraith, M.A., and Pamela Espeland (Minneapolis: Free Spirit Publishing, 1994). More than 900 specific, concrete suggestions help adults help children build Developmental Assets at home, at school, and in the community.

What Young Children Need to Succeed: Working Together to Build Assets from Birth to Age 11 by Jolene L. Roehlkepartain and Nancy Leffert, Ph.D. (Minneapolis: Free Spirit Publishing, 2000). Hundreds of practical, concrete ideas help adults build Developmental Assets for children in four different age groups: birth to 12 months, ages 1–2, 3–5, and 6–11. Includes inspiring true stories from across the United States.

Web sites

Alliance for Youth
www.americaspromise.org
Founded after the Presidents' Summit for America's Future in 1997, this organization is committed to fulfilling five promises to American youth: Every child needs *caring adults, safe places, a healthy start, marketable skills,* and *opportunities to serve.* This collaborative network includes resources, information, and opportunities for involvement.

National Education Association—Help for Parents
www.nea.org/parents
When parents are involved in their children's education, kids do better in school. Here's advice from experts on how to help your child achieve and succeed. Includes guides for parents on understanding testing; helping your child with reading, math, and science; and getting involved in your child's school.

National Mentoring Partnership
www.mentoring.org
The organization provides connections, training, resources, and advice to introduce and support mentoring partnerships. The site is a wealth of information about becoming and finding a mentor.

Search Institute
www.search-institute.org
Through dynamic research and analysis, this independent nonprofit organization works to promote healthy, active, and content youth and communities.

Index

About the Authors

Both Pamela Espeland and Elizabeth Verdick have written many books for children and teens.

Pamela is the coauthor (with Peter L. Benson and Judy Galbraith) of *What Kids Need to Succeed* and *What Teens Need to Succeed* and the author of *Succeed Every Day,* all based on Search Institute's concept of the 40 Developmental Assets. She is the author of *Life Lists for Teens* and the coauthor (with Gershen Kaufman and Lev Raphael) of *Stick Up for Yourself!*

Elizabeth is a children's book writer and editor. She is the author of *Germs Are Not for Sharing, Tails Are Not for Pulling, Teeth Are Not for Biting, Words Are Not for Hurting,* and *Feet Are Not for Kicking,* and coauthor (with Marjorie Lisovskis) of *How to Take the GRRRR Out of Anger* and (with Trevor Romain) of *Stress Can Really Get on Your Nerves* and *True or False? Tests Stink!*

Pamela and Elizabeth first worked together on *Making Every Day Count.* They live in Minnesota with their families and pets.

More Titles in the Adding Assets Series for Kids

By Pamela Espeland and Elizabeth Verdick. Each book is for ages 8–12. *Each $9.95; softcover; two-color illust., 5⅛" x 7".*

People Who Care About You

Kids learn how to build the six Support Assets: Family Support, Positive Family Communication, Other Adult Relationships, Caring Neighborhood, Caring School Climate, and Parent Involvement in Schooling. Stories, tips, and ideas bring them closer to their families and strengthen other important relationships in their lives. *96 pp.*

Helping Out and Staying Safe

Kids learn how to build the four Empowerment Assets: Community Values Children, Children as Resources, Service to Others, and Safety. Stories, tips, and ideas guide them to play useful roles at home and in the community, help others, and feel safer at home, at school, and in their neighborhood. *80 pp.*

Doing and Being Your Best

Kids learn how to build the six Boundaries and Expectations Assets: Family Boundaries, School Boundaries, Neighborhood Boundaries, Adult Role Models, Positive Peer Influence, and High Expectations. Stories, tips, and ideas show them why and how boundaries help them behave in positive, responsible ways. *96 pp.*

Smart Ways to Spend Your Time

Kids learn how to build the four Constructive Use of Time Assets: Creative Activities, Child Programs, Religious Community, and Time at Home. Stories, tips, and ideas promote healthy, constructive, relationship-strengthening interests and activities. *96 pp.*

Knowing and Doing What's Right

Kids learn how to build the six Positive Values Assets: Caring, Equality and Social Justice, Integrity, Honesty, Responsibility, and Healthy Lifestyle. Stories, tips, and ideas help them to make good choices and build positive character traits. *96 pp.*

Other Great Books from Free Spirit

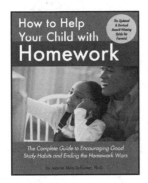

How to Help Your Child with Homework

Every Caring Parent's Guide to Encouraging Good Study Habits and Ending the Homework Wars
Revised and Updated
by Marguerite C. Radencich, Ph.D., and Jeanne Shay Schumm, Ph.D.
Put an end to excuses and arguments while improving your child's school performance. Realistic strategies and proven techniques make homework hassle-free. Includes handouts, resources, and real-life examples. For parents of children ages 6–13.
$14.95; 208 pp.; softcover; 7¹⁄₄" x 9¹⁄₄"

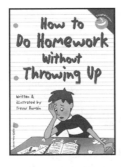

How to Do Homework Without Throwing Up

written and illustrated by Trevor Romain
"Everybody who goes to school does homework . . . and they feel just as sick as you do when they have to do it." Trevor Romain understands how horrible homework can be. Kids will recognize this right away—and as they laugh along with Trevor's jokes, they'll learn how to make a homework schedule, when to do the hardest homework (first!), where to do homework, the benefits of homework, and more.
For ages 8–13.
$8.95; 72 pp.; softcover; illus.; 5¹⁄₈" x 7"

Fast, Friendly, and Easy to Use
www.freespirit.com

Browse the catalog   **Info & extras**   **Many ways to search**   **Quick check-out**   **Stop in and see!**

Our Web site makes it easy to find the positive, reliable resources you need to empower teens and kids of all ages.

The Catalog.
Start browsing with just one click.

Beyond the Home Page.
Information and extras such as links and downloads.

The Search Box.
Find anything superfast.

Request the Catalog.
Browse our catalog on paper, too!

The Nitty-Gritty.
Toll-free numbers, online ordering information, and more.

The 411.
News, reviews, awards, and special events.

 Our Web site is a secure commerce site. All of the personal information you enter at our site—including your name, address, and credit card number—is secure. So you can order with confidence when you order online from Free Spirit!

For a fast and easy way to receive our practical tips, helpful information, and special offers, send your email address to upbeatnews@freespirit.com. View a sample letter and our privacy policy at www.freespirit.com.

1.800.735.7323 • fax 612.337.5050 • help4kids@freespirit.com